Developing ESOL, supporting achievement

NIACE lifelines in adult learning

The *NIACE lifelines in adult learning* series provides straightforward background and information, accessible know-how and useful examples of good practice for all practitioners involved in adult and community learning. Focusing in turn on different areas of adult learning these guides are an essential part of every practitioner's toolkit.

1. **Community education and neighbourhood renewal** – Jane Thompson, ISBN 1 86201 139 7
2. **Spreading the word: reaching out to new learners** – Veronica McGivney, ISBN 1 86201 140 0
3. **Managing community projects for change** – Jan Eldred, ISBN 1 86201 141 9
4. **Engaging black learners in adult and community education** – Lenford White, ISBN 1 86201 142 7
5. **Consulting adults** – Chris Jude, ISBN 1 86201 194 4
6. **Working with young adults** – Carol Jackson, ISBN 1 86201 150 8
7. **Promoting learning** – Kate Malone, ISBN 1 86201 151 6
8. **Evaluating community projects** – Jane Field, ISBN 1 86201 152 4
9. **Working in partnership** – Lyn Tett, ISBN 1 86201 162 1
10. **Working with Asian heritage communities** – David McNulty, ISBN 1 86201 174 5
11. **Learning and community arts** – Tony Fegan, ISBN 1 86201 181 8
12. **Museums and community learning** – Garrick Fincham, ISBN 1 86201 182 6
13. **Developing a needs-based library service** – John Pateman, ISBN 1 86201 183 4
14. **Volunteers and volunteering** – Jan Eldred, ISBN 1 86201 187 7
15. **Sustaining projects for success** – Kay Snowdon, ISBN 1 86201 188 5
16. **Opening up schools for adults** – Judith Summers, ISBN 1 86201 192 3
17. **Befriending learners** – Jane Field, ISBN 1 86201 210 5
18. **Developing literacy: supporting achievement** – Amanda Lindsay and Judith Gawn. ISBN 1 86201 216 4
19. **Developing numeracy: supporting achievement** – Barbara Newmarch, ISBN 1 86201 217 2
20. **Developing ESOL: supporting achievement** – Violet Windsor and Christina Healey, ISBN 1 86201 218 0
21. **Developing embedded literacy, language and numeracy: supporting achievement** – Jan Eldred, ISBN 1 86201 219 9

The Jargon Buster – Yanina Dutton, ISBN 1 86201 215 6

20

niace · lifelines in adult learning

Developing ESOL, supporting achievement

Violet Windsor and Christina Healey

The Regional Achievement Programme is supported by the *Skills for Life* Strategy Unit

Published by the National Institute of
Adult Continuing Education (England and Wales)

21 De Montfort Street
Leicester LE1 7GE
Company registration no. 2603322
Charity registration no. 1002775

First published 2006

The NIACE lifelines in adult learning series is supported by the Adult
and Community Learning Fund. ACLF is funded by the Department
for Education and Skills and managed in partnership by NIACE and
the Basic Skills Agency to develop widening participation in adult learning.

niace
promoting adult learning

NIACE has a broad remit to promote lifelong learning
opportunities for adults. NIACE works to develop
increased participation in education and training,
particularly for those who do not have easy access
because of barriers of class, gender, age, race,
language and culture, learning difficulties and
disabilities, or insufficient financial resources.

www.niace.org.uk

Cataloguing in Publication Data
A CIP record of this title is available from the British Library

Designed and typeset by Boldface
Printed in Great Britain by Russell Press, Nottingham
All photographs courtesy of Sue Parkins, NIACE

ISBN 1 86201 218 0

Contents

Acknowledgements

Thanks must go to:

Suzanne Burdon, Working Links; Brendan Gleeson, Westminster Adult Education Service; Sue Harris and Thea Cross, Adult Education College, Bexley; Vanessa Kent, College of North West London; Sharada Junankar and Angela Ohanugo, Brent Adult and Community Education Service; Philida Schellekens, Independent Language Consultant; Alison Belger and Cathy Glatt, Medway Adult and Community Learning Service; Anne Greenall, Greenwich Community College; Miranda Pestell, Waltham Forest Adult and Community Service; Monica Lucero and Karen Dudley, Tower Hamlets College; Adrian Wilford, North Yorkshire; Lucinda Clark and Julia Racster-Szoztak, Friends Centre, Brighton; Lesley Coles and Barbara Sakyra, Institute of Education, University of London.

Note to the reader

This book has been written primarily for people who are new to teaching ESOL and for practitioners and managers who want an overview of ESOL work. We are grateful to the many people who have commented on the draft and made useful changes.

Wherever possible we have let the learners speak for themselves and used the words actually **spoken** rather than 'correcting' their English. As one learner said, *"We make mistakes but still we have confidence. That's important for us."*

Inspirations: refer to case studies and examples of good practice.

Glossary: the meanings of the words underlined in the text can be found in the glossary.

1 Introduction

In the context of this book ESOL (English for Speakers of Other Languages) refers to the systematic development of English language skills with adults whose first language is not English and who are living and using English in the UK.

ESOL uses many acronyms and we have tried to keep these to a minimum and use the full form for the initial use. Specialist terms are explained in the glossary: some are explained in the text as they are used.

We have concentrated on ESOL provision in adult and community education in order to make the volume of information manageable and to avoid replicating information that exists elsewhere. We also believe that provision for adult learners in the community can develop a wealth of experience and flexibility because it often operates outside large and more formal kinds of organisation. This experience deserves to be acknowledged and we have used it for our 'Inspirations' in particular.

In practice, this has meant that the book focuses on learners over the age of 19 learning on a part-time basis alongside work, looking for jobs or caring for families. Although the focus of their study will be English in everyday use, many learners will want to progress into further learning.

There are advantages as well as disadvantages to being (at least physically) separate from institutionalised education. As Jane Thompson explains in Lifeline 1, *Community Education and Neighbourhood Renewal*, government goals for combating social exclusion offer major opportunities for adult and community education. We hope that ESOL practitioners reading this book will be inspired to look at other volumes in the Lifelines series and link their own work to other, often radical, developments in the field of Adult and Community Learning (ACL).

The time has also come to make ESOL accessible to others involved who come into contact with learners who have ESOL needs. ESOL work is immensely diverse as the range of learners is almost infinite in terms of their cultural backgrounds, first languages, religions and experience of the world. In turn, there are a variety of ways in which these learners' needs can be addressed. There are also differences in terms of how specialists approach the teaching of these learners. This may also make it difficult for other practitioners to feel confident about meeting the needs of students whose first language is not English.

This guide is aimed at practitioners who support or provide English language teaching for adults who live in England and whose first language is not English. It is likely to be particularly useful for the following groups:

- prospective teachers of ESOL, including those in training organisations;
- existing teachers of ESOL to adults who want to review their practice in the light of new initiatives;
- adult education teachers who want to move into ESOL;
- qualified teachers in the schools sector who want to diversify;
- existing teachers of English as a Foreign Language (EFL) who want to teach ESOL to adults in the UK;
- people studying for the new level 2 and 3 qualifications in Literacy, Numeracy and Language (ESOL), e.g City and Guilds 9295;
- Non-specialists involved in this field, such as Trades Union Congress (TUC), Union Learning representatives.

There is growing recognition that ESOL learners should not remain perpetually identified as ESOL learners, and progression from the courses is an increasingly important issue. They are adult learners. This will mean that specialist knowledge and understanding of ESOL will be necessary for staff offering language support and also for subject tutors, advice and guidance staff (see *Skills for Life*).

We aim to offer an introduction to the field of ESOL within adult and community education and to provide a broad account of current developments to further good practice. References to sources of more comprehensive advice and support on key issues are included. We have referred to some sources of support and information in the text and given web site addresses, and there is a complete list at the end.

1 What is ESOL and why does it matter?

What is ESOL?

The government's *Skills for Life* strategy defines ESOL as:

The ability to understand and employ English language in daily activities at home, at work and in the community to achieve one's goals, and to develop one's knowledge and potential.

ESOL matters as part of the adult education curriculum because fluency in English is closely related to the life chances and choices available to people who come here in search of a better life for themselves and their families. The reasons why adults come to Britain are covered more fully in Section 3.

The provision of ESOL courses should meet the needs of individual learners, of the larger community and of employers. It is now also an important part of the government's agenda on citizenship and social inclusion.

The needs of the learner

This is what one learner said:

"I want to learn English and I have to speak fluently so I can say for myself. When I went to speak to my children's teachers or somewhere I needed an interpreter but now I can manage by myself."

The purpose of ESOL teaching is to respond to such needs. However, the *Skills for Life* strategy sets these individual needs within a larger picture.

The needs of employers

In a recent report (Schellekens, 2001), employers identified the following barriers to recruiting second language speakers to jobs:

- inability to speak and/or write English to a sufficient standard;
- written job applications not produced in standard format;
- over-reliance on academic qualifications rather than work experience;
- lack of ability to sell oneself at interview;
- difficulty in establishing equivalence of overseas qualifications.

One learner said:

"I do this course for a job. Because I want a job. I decided when I came to this college for English language why I not do the Care course? I think this easy but it no easy."

The needs of society

Many ESOL learners do not have a problem with the idea of fitting into British society.

"We live in England now, we must learn English." (ESOL learner)

The government has recently introduced new regulations for those who wish to settle in the UK and those who wish to become UK citizens which will have an impact on ESOL provision. However, the potential conflict between an approach to teaching and learning that focuses on assimilation into UK life and an approach which recognises and values diverse cultural experiences, beliefs and lifestyles is not one that ESOL teachers can avoid.

By putting the burden of studying the language and institutions of the host community onto the immigrant alone, we risk becoming a nation where the local population remains ignorant both of the reasons behind immigration, and the economic and cultural benefits to the country that it provides. The ESOL teacher and the citizenship tutor (a new breed – it could be you!) risk becoming important to the seeker-after-citizenship for all the wrong reasons. Fiona Frank, 'Backwards to the Future,' Basic Skills Bulletin (November 2003)

Personal fulfilment

There is a danger that approaches which focus solely on English for work and citizenship can ignore the motivation of the individual learner. Here, two different learners express their reasons for attending ESOL classes:

> **"I improve my English for myself because when my children are doing their homework, I help them. It's very important for me. In future I want to get a job."**

> "I have to thank you for this most illuminating lesson.
> I have wished all my life to be an educated man, but
> until now the need to provide for my family has made it
> impossible. I left school very young. God has blessed my
> work and enabled me to provide for my sons the
> education I could not have... Now I have a teacher, I am
> sure I can begin to attain my life's ambition."
> Molteno (1987) p.1

All of the above has implications for the approaches that are adopted in the classroom and will affect course content, judgements about what counts as achievement for learners and how the tutor interacts with learners.

A history of the provision of ESOL in England

Alongside the history of settlement in the UK there is an accompanying history of ESOL teaching going back at least to the beginning of the twentieth century. However, this teaching was marked by extreme inconsistency in provision in different parts of the country. Indeed, some Local Education Authorities (LEAs) claimed to have "a policy of not having a policy" towards the educational needs of adult immigrants and refugees. Others had developed excellent learning opportunities.

The 1990s saw major structural changes in post-16 education which resulted in a weakened role for LEAs. The advisory teams of inspectors (who were often the key to providing resources and training for ESOL tutors) were gradually disbanded. The 1992 Further and Higher Education Act only required LEAs to make provision for adult learners and this resulted in the demise of adult and community education in some authorities. Some LEAs amalgamated their adult centres with local FE colleges, others franchised the work with adults, so that ESOL work was often carried forward into what became large local colleges.

As the opportunities for ESOL learning were being reduced, especially in community settings, there were increasing numbers of refugees coming from Somalia, Eritrea, Sierra Leone, former Yugoslavia and Sri Lanka in particular. These new arrivals were frequently competing for places in an ESOL class with each other and with adults from the settled communities of the New Commonwealth. There was far more demand for ESOL places than those being provided. Simultaneously, some LEAs and colleges were reducing spending on adult learners. Staff were made redundant or moved into other teaching. It was not a time of much growth, although the training sector continued to expand particularly when courses were combined with Information and Communication Technology (ICT).

When the Labour government came into power in 1997, it made an explicit commitment to education and particularly among those sections of the population who faced economic and social disadvantage. An investigation into the literacy and numeracy needs of adults was undertaken, which resulted in the Moser Report (1999). Officially entitled *A Fresh Start*, the report lead to the development of the governments Skills for Life strategy to tackle those needs. However, government policy was concerned with tackling more than disadvantage and social exclusion. The need to have a population educated to similar standards as our European neighbours was of major importance. The Moser Report focussed on literacy and numeracy. To address the gaps, a number of working parties were set up.

An ESOL working party was formed and its recommendations formed the basis for the report *Breaking the Language Barriers* (2000). The report estimated that between half and one million places were required to meet the needs of learners (this is thought to be an underestimate).

They are not a homogeneous or static group but a diverse and dynamic one, which encompasses both long settled minority ethnic communities and groups of refugees who have arrived in this country more recently. Potential learners range from those who may lack basic literacy and numeracy skills in their own language to those with a high level of education and qualifications in their home country, and from those who are not keen to re-enter formal education to those who are highly motivated to learn.

In all cases, their principle need is to improve their command of English. All the evidence suggests that lack of fluency in English is a very significant factor in poverty and underachievement in many minority ethnic communities, and a major barrier to employment and workplace opportunities and further and higher education. (DfES, p. 1, 2000)

In 2001 the government published its *Skills for Life* strategy. In 2002 another strategy, *Success for All*, was launched to address issues of quality and responsiveness in the sector. The Adult Basic Skills Strategy Unit (ABSSU) was established and a regional support structure for Basic Skills was developed through the local Learning and Skills Councils (LSCs).

What's the difference between ESOL and EFL?

The following are the personal experiences of two practitioners used to teaching EFL abroad who then made the transition to teaching ESOL in the UK:

"...we quickly found out that there is a significant difference between the two and that we would have to make huge adjustments to our teaching... They fall into two main categories: those concerning the learners and learners and those concerning the methodology." (Burdon and Guneri, 2003, page 2 of iatefl ES(O)L SIG newsletter)

ESOL learners' previous experiences of education can be fantastically varied. Some may have had few opportunities for formal education, some may have very high-level qualifications. Their way of life may be very different as well as their religion. The EFL learner on the other hand, is far more likely to come from a Western educational background and be familiar with Western cultural references.

The trained EFL teacher has much to bring to ESOL learners but has to be able to put his/her knowledge about language and the skills of language teaching into a wider context. This includes language teaching into a wider context. This includes not only the contemporary context of the *Skills for Life* initiative but also the historical context of adult and community learning with its regard for the autonomous adult learner and the global context of migration and resettlement.

"...there is so much more to teaching ES(O)L students apart from teaching the language. We switched from EFL to ES(O)L three years ago and have enjoyed every minute of it. The rewards from a personal and pedagogical point of view have been immeasurable and we recommend it unreservedly." (Burdon and Guneri, 2003, p. 2)

3 ESOL learners

Who are the ESOL learners?

Anyone settled in the UK who wants to develop their English skills may find their way to an ESOL class. Alongside refugees and asylum seekers are other ESOL learners. Although the former New Commonwealth communities are well established in Britain there are still spouses and dependants coming to join families settled here. Among communities from India, Pakistan and Bangladesh, brides and bridegrooms from 'home' are particularly valued because they reinforce old ties. When the new spouse arrives in Britain they may find they need ESOL classes to learn or improve spoken English. There are also people from European Union coun--tries working here who want to learn English for a variety of reasons: for example Portuguese men and women working in the hotel industry. There are spouses of overseas students and overseas spouses married to UK citizens. Another new group is the seasonal fruit pickers, for example, from Eastern Europe, whose employers may request on site classes.

Most ESOL learners underestimate the amount of time required to reach a level of linguistic competence that will get them into further study or a job. Philida Schelleken's (2002) research suggests that to reach the equivalent of Level 2 competence in English, beginners need 1,765 hours of study. It is not difficult to appreciate why some learners give up and why many teachers have to work hard to keep learners motivated.

Many languages, many peoples – an overview of settlement in the UK

Different approaches to ESOL are influenced by the history of settlement in the UK. It is important that everyone working with ESOL learners understands the different reasons for migration and the different histories of communities settled here.

Britain has always attracted people from around the world. Many thousands have come as refugees, escaping war, famine or persecution. Many more were invited because they had much-needed skills. Although newcomers have often been treated with suspicion, their contribution to life and culture in Britain has been enormous.

An historical perspective challenges the myth of a monolingual Britain. The very diverse groups of settlers in twenty first-century Britain will have had three main reasons for coming: work, refuge and family.

> **"They [the organisation] communicate their expectation effectively and positively, and make them explicit to all involved."** DfES (2002) p. 9

Work

In times of economic boom Britain looks abroad for sources of cheap labour. In the 1950s and 1960s many people from the Caribbean and South Asia were encouraged to come and work in the Health Service, public transport and manual industries. Many only intended to stay for a short while and then return but as their children were born in the UK and as more old people stayed here, the original workers found that, whether they liked it or not, they were committed to staying here for the long term.

Few of those refugees and immigrants who had been employed in their home country were able to find a job of equivalent skill and status. Therefore, they frequently took work below their level of skill but where their command of English was felt to be acceptable. This pattern of employment continues today, although the workers' countries of origin are always changing.

Asylum

While it could be said that those workers had some degree of choice in moving to Britain, many who come seeking refuge often have no choice at all. It is no longer possible for them to stay in their own country. In the last hundred years or so people have sought asylum in UK from many countries, including Russia, Hungary, Uganda, Cyprus, Kurdistan, Iran, Iraq, Bosnia, Eritrea, Somalia, Congo, Ivory Coast, Zimbabwe, Sri Lanka and Kosovo. For example, during the long war between Eritrea and Ethiopia, people from both sides of the conflict came to the UK in the 1980s and 90s.

Family

The pull of family starts to have an effect once a community begins to settle and others from that community come to the UK. Some come to marry the original settlers. Parents come to join their sons and daughters who are now settled here.

> **"One way to tackle prejudice is to adopt a constant, conscious policy of inclusion."** DfES (2002) p. 10

> **"Students who are encouraged to believe in themselves and take responsibility for their own learning tend to do better. They are also empowered."** DfES (2002) p. 6

Children left in the care of other family members (sometimes to enable the mother to continue working here) join their parents once they reach school age. Although the countries of origin may change, this pattern is likely to continue in the future.

The movement of peoples from one part of the world to another is likely to increase rather than decrease. Far too often, new settlers face hostility and racism from the communities in which they have settled. Some learners have bitter experiences of racist behaviour and attitudes, which will have affected them.

Removing the barriers

Why is language perceived as a barrier? Our minority languages and communities are, in other contexts, majorities. If modern Britain is to become a truly inclusive society, adult education needs to become more proactive over its relationship with those learners whose first language is not English. The historic situation seems to be one of parallel provision: publicly funded courses for 'the disadvantaged' and privately funded ones, which are theoretically open to all who can pay the fees. A commitment to inclusion means improving the quality and quantity of ESOL provision.

Removing the Barriers (DfES, 2002) is a video-based training pack for schools but its message is applicable to all education organisations. Committed adult educators should have little difficulty in relating to its core values and these values may help ESOL staff to develop work with learners on other courses. These values are:

- high expectations;
- a positive organisational culture and ethos (leadership and a 'mission');
- academic support;
- tackling prejudice and promoting inclusion.

> **"Diversity should be valued and celebrated. It should be seen as an opportunity – not an excuse for underachievement."** DfES (2002) p. 6

4 ESOL within the *Skills for Life* strategy

Skills for Life

Skills for Life is the government's national strategy to improve adult literacy, numeracy and language (ESOL) skills. It incorporates many of the recommendations of *Breaking the Language Barriers*. The *Skills for Life* strategy was planned to build on the literacy and numeracy strategies in schools and to link with broader government social policies.

It is estimated that there are up to one million adults in England and Wales who do not speak English as their first language and have language and literacy needs. A specialist curriculum for ESOL, materials relating to language and citizenship and a teacher training programme are all part of the strategy.

The Skills for Life strategy involves:

- putting in place meaningful professional and career development opportunities for those involved in delivering programmes in the three skills areas;
- developing qualifications for adult learners based on the curriculum frameworks.

The *Skills for Life* strategy includes curriculum organisers, tutors and learners. It is to be hoped that senior managers will embrace the idea that all staff in an organisation need a thorough understanding of and commitment to the strategy. This is more likely to happen in organisations that have a strong belief in inclusion.

To keep up to date on *Skills for Life* go to: www.dfes.gsi.gov.uk/readwriteplus. To find out more about the adult ESOL Core Curriculum go to: www.dfes.gov.uk/curriculum_esol

ESOL and citizenship

New Home Office language requirements for applicants seeking UK citizenship have come into force which will impact on providers and on learners.

In September 2002, the then Home Secretary, David Blunkett, announced the Government's intention to make becoming a British citizen a more meaningful event. An advisory group was appointed by the government, chaired by Sir Bernard Crick to consider "how best to achieve the Government's plans to promote language skills and practical knowledge about the United Kingdom for those seeking to become British citizens." Among the recommendations of this Advisory Group, was a proposal for applicants for citizenship to follow a programme of studies and take an assessment of English language skills. In July 2004, the Home Office stated that the standard of knowledge of the English language which applicants for naturalisation needed was to be defined as ESOL Entry 3. This means that anybody wishing to apply for citizenship who has English language skills below Entry 3 will need to attend a course to bring them to the required level. NIACE recognises that there are challenges for providers here in terms of:

- insufficient ESOL provision and current waiting lists;
- the capacity of the sector to meet expectations of those eligible to come forward for citizenship;
- the current shortage of teaching expertise in ESOL and the capacity of language teachers;
- limited access to e-learning, particularly in the voluntary and community sector.

NIACE and LLU+ have been funded by the DfES and the Home Office to define the broad areas of content for two citizenship programmes that will develop learners' knowledge of life in the UK and support application for citizenship. Together with the London Language and Literacy Unit, NIACE has also developed ESOL citizenship learning materials for learners working towards Entry 1, 2 or 3 which have been piloted with 18 ESOL providers in England.

For more information about the ESOL and citizenship project, go to: www.niace. org.uk/Research/BasicSkills/Projects/ESOL-Citizenship. The web page also includes a link to the Home Office website which provides information on Home Office language requirements for citizenship.

ESOL in the community

The following case studies are examples of the ways in which providers and tutors can respond to the varying needs of individual learners.

INSPIRATIONS

Ethiopian community class

The Ethiopian Community of Britain works in partnership with the outreach arm of the College of North West London to host an ESOL class. The class is open to all but attracts mainly Ethiopian, Somali and Eritrean learners from all over London.

Although the groups tend to be very varied in their level of attainment in English language skills, learners still prefer to come here first before possibly moving on to a more formally graded college course.

The mixture of learners poses particular challenges for the teacher. Despite the "spiky profiles" of the learners she always tries to begin and end with a whole group activity and always chooses one over-riding theme for the lesson which will interest and include everyone. Listening and speaking activities are often done as a whole group but with different tasks set. For example, Entry 2 Level learners develop their skills through a short passage in continuous prose while Entry 1 Level learners match sentences that they had previously heard spoken and beginners work on recognising the initial letter sounds in words which are significant to the theme of the lesson. The learners respond very positively to this and work together very well.

LEA adult education service
Medway Adult and Community Learning Service (MACLS)
This study particularly illustrates learner support and achievement.
ESOL provision in Medway developed out of the Parosi (neighbourhood-based) scheme which largely used volunteer tutors. It now has a substantial and wide-ranging programme that includes community-based courses as well as a wide range of accredited and non-accredited courses. Core funding is through the Learning and Skills Council (LSC), supplemented by successful project bids. In 2003, there were over 1,700 enrolments by 650 ESOL learners.

The ESOL programme offers a range of English classes: general English; Listening, Speaking and Pronunciation; ESOL through Letter Writing; ESOL through Office Skills; ESOL through Driving Theory; and ESOL through Practical Crafts (e.g. sewing and floristry). Classes range from Entry Level 1 to Level 1. External accreditation is through Pitman ESOL exams, Trinity Spoken exams and LCCI Business English. There are several Guided Learning sessions each week which are on a 'drop in' basis, for learners to practise specific skills which they have chosen or to practise for exams. Before each set of exams, short practice classes are run so learners become familiar with the requirements of the exam.

Learners in the main centres have the opportunity to attend a formal review once a term and receive a lot of one-to-one attention. All learners have a learning record, which they maintain for each session and discuss with another ESOL tutor at the review session. It is evident from the tutors' written comments on course work that learners are given sound advice on correcting errors, and that this is given in ways which encourage learners to take control of their learning.

There is a well-established and growing team of experienced tutors, including bilingual tutors. The Curriculum Leaders continue to do some teaching and several staff are now involved in teaching on Level 4 *Skills for Life* professional accreditation and university courses (e.g. Trinity TESOL, Cert Ed., and PGCE as well as in-house ESOL training).

A Punjabi-speaking tutor is the programme's Education Guidance worker who is the only paid guidance worker in the service. Several years ago, the team requested formal training in educational guidance for her. Initially the request was refused, the costs were high for an adult education organisation, but she was subsequently helped to access professional training and is due to complete Level 4 training in summer 2004. She is a crucial part of the ESOL team and both ESOL learners and enquirers from the local resident minority ethnic communities are referred to her. This results in provision which is available to all minority ethnic learners rather than contained in an ESOL-only facility. She also gives advice to refugees who may have few ESOL needs but want their existing qualifications matched to their English equivalent and to be referred to vocational and professional courses elsewhere.

There are regular team meetings, everyone knows their role within the team, ensuring that new members of staff are integrated into the work of the team as a whole. In 2000, tutors requested support and training so they could have more knowledge of how to support and integrate ESOL learners with special educational needs into the provision. This became part of their professional development and now means that learners with learning difficulties and disabilities are not excluded from the main programme of provision.

The two main centres have a crèche, a chair lift, and good refreshment facilities. The main teaching rooms on both sites have computers for student use. Induction loops are available at both main centres. The Learner Support Fund (LSF) helps individual learners, including the payment of exam fees, travel and childcare expenses. Two community venues have childcare assistants also paid for by LSF.

The service is developing embedded ESOL work in Creative and Practical Crafts, Driving Theory and ICT. All these courses have been successful and have sometimes led to unexpected developments. Following several successful short-term projects ESOL expanded into local community venues and after the end of the projects has maintained classes in most of them. These include three Gurdwaras (Sikh temples), a mosque, a Chinese Association, two primary schools, and a Healthy Living Centre (for an Elderly Chinese Group). ESOL classes also take place in a fruit-packing factory.

Participation in other activities which support progression is encouraged and all learners on *Skills for Life* courses are eligible for a 20% discount voucher when they join a non-*Skills for Life* course.

Student attendance and retention have improved dramatically and this is attributed to the dedication of tutors and to learners seeing that they are achieving, particularly now they can relate to the framework of the ESOL Curriculum. *"Learners are achieving small steps within this framework and their goals have meaning for them."*

(Curriculum leader)

INSPIRATIONS

Differentiation in an inner-city ESOL class

In an adult education class at Entry Level 2 in inner London, the tutor was very aware of the differences between the students even though they were all nominally at the same level. The differences identified included:

- differences of experience, particularly in the context of the topic of the lesson which was 'finding a job';
- differences of language background;
- differences of attainment in English;
- differences of learning style – some learners liked to learn through visual modes like drawing, others liked to move around or "act out" the language they were learning, others liked to learn by transferring their knowledge of language "rules" from other languages they had studied.

By recognising and respecting these differences the tutor was able to show that he was treating the learners as autonomous adults who could take control of their own learning. Within the overriding topic for the class there was often a choice of activity and learners were encouraged to move around and to work with many different people. By supporting this variety the tutor was providing an opportunity for learners to be more in control of their own learning and the students flourished, as did their ability to support and encourage each other.

Different models of provision

It is important that learners have access to advice and guidance to support them in making informed choices about what sort of provision best meets their needs. When designing provision the important thing to remember is to focus on the learner's motivation and to ask yourselves "What is the learner learning from this course?" and "What is the precise purpose of this course?" It is vital that all courses are designed to include English language skills (mapped to the ESOL Core Curriculum), even when the content is embedded in another subject. There is a plethora of models but here are a selection of the most common:

i Courses organised according to level

Many courses are organised according to the language levels of different learners. On these courses, learners are taught the four skills of reading, writing, listening and speaking, and sessions may be based on a series of topics relevant to learners' lives and negotiated with them. Courses of this type probably form the bulk of most ESOL provision. In some organisations, a course lasts a term and in others, a year. It is important to provide a wide range of possibilities to suit learners other commitments. As with all adult learners, family commitments and health issues can affect attendance but ESOL learners may also have additional difficulties with immigration status or housing. Some programmes run termly courses courses but there are issues around proving achievement, especially if outcomes are accredited.

ii Embedded ESOL

These are courses where learners learn the subject matter, the specific subject vocabulary and grammatical patterns of English simultaneously. The ESOL tutor is adept at identifying, analysing and teaching the communication and literacy skills of the subject in co-operation with the subject tutor who, whilst taking responsibility for the subject content, helps the ESOL tutor understand the knowledge and understanding of the subject. For example, learners on a Health and Social Care course with embedded ESOL who are learning how to resuscitate a casualty will read information from St John's Ambulance Brigade. At the same time they will practice reading instructions and learn specific vocabulary such as *compressions*, *blood pressure* and *fracture*. As one tutor said, *"My students are really keen to get into nursing so studying English in the context of health and social care is a real motivator."*

The ideal is for embedded ESOL courses to benefit from the expertise of both a subject specialist and a language specialist (e.g. ICT, plumbing, horticulture). However, embedded courses may sometimes be taught by a single tutor in both areas. The resulting content can motivate learners who can learn language and subject knowledge in a meaningful way without feeling they have to first learn English to a particular level.

These sorts of courses can also help learners to join other adult education courses. However, it is important that appropriate support exists for the learners as they progress. Organisations should have practices in place which address people's learning needs but also ensure that they feel included and welcomed:

"Can you imagine the situation for a Bengali woman from our ESOL and Sewing course who wants to join a group, which is effectively a sewing club for English women?" (Observer comment)

iii Work-based learning

Courses for finding employment and work-based learning are specialist forms of provision that require ESOL tutors to be thoroughly familiar with the demands and expectations of employers, particularly about language. The language work should be based around the tasks and communication practices in the job. It is useful for tutors to work with union learning reps to recruit people to courses because many workers can feel anxious about revealing their difficulties to their employers.

iv Family learning

Family classes often involve parents and children learning a subject together. Unless there is specific ESOL input these will not qualify for ESOL funding although they may complement ESOL provision.

v Fast-track

Fast-track or intensive courses which usually revise knowledge of the grammatical forms or structures of English, possibly using a thematic approach. These are useful for students who have a lot of passive knowledge which the tutor can activate. Some English for Specific Purposes (ESP) courses may use this approach and graft the content knowledge required by higher education e.g. for doctors, nurses, business people, onto a structural framework. They would probably aim to get students to about Level 2 by the end of the course. Intensive courses are very important for refugees who want to find work quickly.

vi Classes in the community

Community-based classes, often women or men only, may be held in a building belonging to aparticular community group. An ESOL community development worker will often support the host group to identify the purpose of the course. These courses often provide an important link and access to other ESOL provision. Other NIACE Lifelines, like *Working with Asian Heritage Communities and Promoting Learning* are useful sources of advice. This is what one adult education manager said:

"We got some extra funding and that gave us the chance to really develop our community based ESOL. We've still got classes running with three of the local faith and community groups and it really makes a difference when ESOL staff go into community premises – it's a reversal of the usual situation. The [English] tutor speaks some Punjabi and she wears a shalwar-kameez (Asian form of the trouser suit with a scarf or chunni) and it isn't a token thing. Some of the women moved around the furniture in the classroom on their own initiative to make the most of the natural light. It's the first time students have done something like that and I think it's great. They tell their tutor what they want to learn too, and they're really making good progress."

vii Advanced English

Access to GCSE English or Advanced English courses may be run for a mixture of ESOL learners and first language learners who do not have GCSE English. The courses usually lead onto preparation for GCSE. The advantage for ESOL learners is that employers in particular can make comparisons with people who have been educated in the UK. Learners also enjoy studying alongside adults whose first language is English

viii Informal groups in the community

Not all potential ESOL learners are interested in learning English to a high standard but want to practise and maintain social and functional forms of English. These groups often provide social support and contact with other statutory agencies and community groups. The Dartford Women's *Milun* (a Punjabi word meaning 'gathering') was established in 1985 by the ESOL organiser with the support of a Social Services community worker. As a result, Social Services developed bilingual services for Punjabi speakers.

An Adult and Community Learning Fund (ACLF) funded project attracted new learners by resurrecting handicraft skills within the local Asian communities, such as embroidery. New learners came into the centre to do traditional craft-work but when they saw the machine patchwork going on in the mainstream class next door they all wanted to try it. We ended up putting on three courses. As a result we've had closer links with Creative Studies. We've put on a course called Practical Studies with OCN accreditation. It isn't patchwork this year but the title means we can change the craft according to demand. We've mapped it to the ESOL core curriculum
(ESOL manager)

ix Independent learning facilities, libraries, computers

Many ESOL programmes face demand for classes that far exceeds their capacity. However, because ESOL learners generally do not experience the inhibitions and lack of confidence that many adult literacy learners face, some enjoy studying independently either in conjunction with or in addition to their course. For them, libraries are an obvious learning resource.

x Language Support

Language support may be offered to ESOL learners who are enrolled on vocational courses which do not benefit from an embedded approach. In this case, the ESOL tutor provides add-on classes to help learners get to grips with the subject content. These may be on a one-to-one or small group basis.

Whatever provision is being offered it is important to have clear, written information available to support verbal advice, particularly if learners are being signposted by another provider.

ICT and ESOL

Using computers provide opportunities for accessing new resources and activities and as a teaching and learning tool can be highly motivating. Most ESOL learners will welcome opportunities to use ICT to access online activities, such as e-mail and the internet and work on their English, for example to improve text presentation.

> "We're doing ESOL through the Internet and emails. ICT is a growing thing. As tutors get more computer literate they'll use it and they see the benefits. We've had a Yahoo tutor group for a year and six months ago I set up a student group. I've posted up useful sites for learning English according to level and subject and linking in with Skillswise (BBC basic skills resource) so students can access exercises for themselves. Another thing I did with my group was as an alternative to doing timetables, which they knew, was to get them to access flight times so they could check when relatives were arriving. That went down really well and it was another way of practising the language for time.' **(MACLS organiser)**

> For a few years now we've been running 'ESOL through Driving Theory'. It combines reading skills, listening skills, speaking and discussion. We use a CD-ROM with driving theory questions which links images to reading. There's also a planned walk round Rochester looking at road signs. We also set a mock test. It really brings the language to life. **(MACLS organiser)**

Useful resources

A useful resource, full of practical advice, is *Using laptop computers to develop basic skills: a handbook for practitioners* (BSA and NRDC, 2003). It includes ideas not only on using laptops but also on developing ICT. There are also exemplar materials (mapped to the literacy and numeracy core curricula) and an accompanying CD-ROM with hyperlinks to the other sites. It is obtainable free of charge by downloading it from NRDC website.

The Training Adult Literacy, ESOL and Numeracy Tutors (TALENT) website is another very useful resources: http://www.talent.ac.uk

The *Working with refugees and asylum seekers pack* (DfES, 2003) provides further details of useful websites. These include activities for learners, resources for tutors and learners and translation websites. These websites could be used by tutors and learners for a range of purposes, such as downloading ESOL exercises, and finding current advice and information. It is available from DfES: dfes@prolog.uk.com

London Online is a combined project and course. It is part of an initiative to train ESOL teachers paired with multimedia developers from further and adult community education to produce online interactive ESOL materials. The materials are available on: www.talent/londononline

5 Working as an ESOL tutor

Who are the ESOL teachers?

As a result of the Skills for Life strategy, more people are being trained as ESOL tutors. There is no such thing as a 'typical' ESOL tutor.

'M' came to the UK from Mauritius at the age of 15. He did not find it easy at first but eventually managed to achieve a degree as a mature student. He now teaches ESOL full time. He says that his early language experiences in Mauritius using a range of French and English Creoles and his experiences on arrival in the UK as a 'black' person in a white society both help him to build an empathy with his learners.

'V' was born in the UK into a large African Caribbean family. She did well at school and had a successful career in the civil service. However, when she was in her 40s she decided she needed to do something more people-centred. She started becoming interested in the many different people and languages in her South Birmingham neighbourhood. She took an initial ESOL teacher training course at her local college and now teaches ESOL part time in the evenings. Every week she draws on her experience of life in the inner city to plan her lessons.

'L' was very good at languages at school and took a joint degree in French and Spanish. Her interest in Spanish and Latino culture drew her to work as a volunteer with the South American community and this led on to a career in ESOL.

'C''s interest in Islamic art and poetry drew him in to contact with the UK's Iranian ex-patriot community and so on into a wider interest in ESOL.

'E' taught English for a year in Japan after graduating in the UK. He attempted to learn to read Japanese and the experience of battling with a whole new script and mode of literacy inspired him to think more about the process of language learning and to train as an ESOL teacher when he returned to the UK.

What qualifications are needed to work in ESOL?

The qualifications you need depend on the context in which you are working. There are now qualifications at Level 2 for volunteers (also used for frontline staff who are often the first point of contact); Level 3 for classroom assistants and Level 4 for classroom teachers who are responsible for the teaching and learning. Each level has its own particular purpose and it is not necessary that someone should cover all the three levels.

Giving tutors professional recognition through a framework that is accepted and understood in the post-16 sector is a major breakthrough and should result in a more professional workforce. Although the *Skills for Life* qualifications currently apply to new entrants, it is obviously wise to take advantage of opportunities for Continuous Professional Development (CPD). Accreditation of Prior Learning (APL) is also being developed for experienced teachers.

Level 2

Those who wish to become volunteers or who would like a foundation in ESOL work will need to attend a Level 2 course which will lead to a recognised qualification such as City and Guilds 9295 'Certificate of Adult Learner Support'. This qualification has three units which are taken progressively. Unit 1 is externally set and marked and requires volunteers to demonstrate a thorough and practical understanding of the issues underpinning *Skills for Life* both locally and nationally. Unit 2 requires demonstrating through practical application the issues of support, including *Access for All*. Unit 3 is about acquiring the basic knowledge of ESOL. Anyone doing this unit must have, or be simultaneously working for, a Level 2 qualification in English language. Both units 2 and 3 require contact with learners and a tutor who will support and direct the volunteer.

Level 3

Anyone wanting to support ESOL learners must gain a qualification at Level 3. This could be a vocational tutor who has ESOL learners in their class or someone working as a classroom assistant in an ESOL setting. Courses are accredited by OCNW, OCR and City and Guilds.

Level 4

A good starting point is a Cambridge ESOL Certificate (CELTA) or the Trinity Certificate. These are both offered on integrated courses where the course participants learn how to analyse language for the purposes of teaching as well as learning how to teach it.

"From September 2003 all new entrants to the teaching profession who wish to specialize in teaching ESOL will be required to enrol on FENTO [now LLU UK] approved programmes that meet the requirements of the ESOL Subject Specifications at level 4 and lead to the new level 4 Certificate for ESOL Subject Specifications and those who wish to support ESOL learning must work towards the Level 3 Certificate for ESOL Subject Support... There are currently no requirements for existing teachers and those who support the teaching and learning of...ESOL to obtain the new specialist certificate... However it is expected that over time, in the interests of parity, equal opportunities and in the light of the requirements of the statutory inspection regime, existing adult ESOL teachers will take up oppor-

tunities to obtain the new specialist qualifications as part of their continuing professional development". (DfES, 2003, p. 5)

This subject specific qualification can be achieved either alongside a generic teacher training qualification or following on from a recognised Cert Ed. or PGCE.

Starting off

There is a lot to learn to become a good ESOL teacher but a good starting place is your own personal experience and interests, whether of growing up bilingual, of learning another language or of forced migration. But this is only a start. Personal experience has to be supplemented by reading (see the resources section), meeting other people, learning from colleagues and most of all by learning from the learners. The capacity to listen to learners in an informed and open way is probably the best ability that any ESOL teacher or support tutor can have.

This essential, sometimes informal, learning will then be supplemented by systematic study. Once on training courses, teachers will gain a good grasp of the theories and structures of the English language.

This can be gained by attendance at an approved training course supported by guided reading. local Professional Development Centres (PDC's) offer training. A number of Higher Education Institutions (HEIs) offer courses matching the subject specifications. These must be approved by the Further Education National Training Organisation (FENTO).

ESOL teachers and English language use

The knowledge and understanding of the English language that an ESOL teacher needs is set out in the subject specifications for teachers of ESOL. The final section of the ESOL subject specifications deal with the personal levels of competence in English language use that are necessary for a fully trained professional ESOL teacher. The skills are divided into: speaking and listening, reading and writing.

On a Level 4 teacher training course, spoken English will be assessed by the trainees' ability to present seminar papers to their colleagues and also to communicate effectively with their learners in the classroom. Being bilingual is considered a tremendous asset and many highly successful teachers have English as their second, third or fourth language.

If there are any concerns about whether a prospective trainee's spoken and written English reaches the required level to become an ESOL practitioner, the course tutors will assess his/her personal English use against the standards in the subject specifications. Sometimes it is useful to take an advanced English course either before or alongside the training course so that the trainee feels confident to deal with the demands of assignments and teaching.

Subject knowledge and teaching ability

All ESOL teachers will need to eventually acquire a sound knowledge of English language structures alongside their communicative use in 'real life'; this is the key for ESOL practitioners. For example, a teacher might want to teach learners how to ask directions and say "Excuse me, where can I get a bus to the train station?" The teacher needs to understand how questions are formed. In addition s/he must know how to help learners achieve appropriate intonation and pronunciation in those phrases. These skills and many others are covered by specialist ESOL teacher training courses.

The content of these courses extends well beyond learning about language to include generic issues, i.e. skills that are necessary for all teachers. Tutors will learn how to plan a structured and appropriate programme of learning and how to plan individual sessions that have defined and clear outcomes. Planning and designing a course, particularly one that integrates other content, is difficult and tutors should be provided with advice and training in order to enable them to plan and deliver their courses effectively. Having planned and taught the learners, the tutor needs to be able to evaluate her/his teaching making full use of feedback from learners, observers and managers. The subsequent insights should lead to adapting learning programmes and methodologies. An important part of the learning loop Is to give feedback to learners on their learning to help them progress in their learning and support them in working towards achieving recognised qualifications if appropriate.

Using resources

In 2003, the DfES, with the aid of ESOL specialists, produced learner materials with tutor notes and audio CDs. For information about these, visit the DfES *readwriteplus* website (http://www.dfes.gov.uk/readwriteplus/). In the last five years there has been a huge expansion of materials that can be used with ESOL learners. Previously, ESOL tutors became very skilled at adapting commercial materials developed for the EFL market. Nowadays many EFL textbooks are mapped to the ESOL Core Curriculum and somewhat adapted to ESOL learners needs. Anyone working with ESOL learners needs to know how to make the best use of resources to plan interesting and appropriate lessons and it is useful to know that there are resources written specifically for ESOL learners. These may not be always currently available but a look in a local ESOL resources cupboard may reveal some of the books listed in the Resources section of this publication.

Anyone wanting more comprehensive information about the qualifications framework can download the full document from:
http://www.dfes.gov.uk/readwriteplus/qualityandtraining

For information about training and professional development opportunities in your region contact your local Learning and Skills Council who should be able to put you in touch with your local *Skills for Life* Professional Development Centre or other providers offering specialist ESOL teacher qualifications.

TALENT (training adult literacy, ESOL and numeracy tutors) is the London online community of adult basic skills teaching. It carries information for people who want to become adult literacy, ESOL and numeracy teachers, materials for teachers and teacher trainers, news items and a noticeboard for views and comments. The TALENT website is useful for those outside London as well. Visit: www.talent.ac.uk

6 The Adult ESOL Core Curriculum

The purpose of the ESOL core curriculum is:

"...to clarify the skills, knowledge and understanding that learners need in order to reach the national standards". (Adult ESOL Core Curriculum, 2001, p. 2)

The Curriculum Framework gives suggestions for the content of ESOL teaching. These are only indicative – what mainly determines the curriculum should be the interests and motivations of the learners in a particular class.

The Core Curriculum is a tool for the ESOL teacher to use. It is not expected that every learning activity will be matched to the Curriculum. It provides guidance on the range of items that a learner will need to address. It maps the stages that learners are likely to go through as they develop competence in their additional language.

The Curriculum distinguishes between the skills of speaking, listening, writing and reading although the point is made strongly that learning activities usually develop more than one skill at a time. Excellent examples of <u>integrated activities</u> are included in the Curriculum document. Each of these different skills is described at five different levels: Entry 1, Entry 2, Entry 3, Level 1 and Level 2. Each level comprises a wide band of differing attainments. Level 1 is equivalent to GCSE grades D and E, Level 2 is equivalent to GCSE A*, A, B and C grades.

It is worth noting here that the majority of learners are reportedly in Entry Levels 1 and 2. In many organisations, however, it often becomes useful to distinguish between complete beginners and those with some English. Some institutions have decided to accommodate sub-levels within each level, e.g. Entry level A and Entry level B.

In addition to the ESOL Core Curriculum, there is a Literacy Core Curriculum and a Numeracy Core Curriculum. Strictly speaking, adult literacy is distinguished from ESOL in that learners attending literacy courses are often native English speakers and fully fluent in spoken English.

Within the development of *Skills for Life* adult literacy and ESOL have been drawn more closely together. However, the Curriculum Standards for each subject have separate roots. The Adult Literacy Core Curriculum draws heavily on practice in the schools sector and the National Curriculum. The Adult ESOL Core Curriculum standards require that tutors have an in-depth understanding of how the English language works and that they can employ a range of appropriate methods of communication in order plan integrated activities. This means that the language knowledge required for literacy tutors is not the same as the linguistic based knowledge needed by ESOL practitioners.

The ESOL Core Curriculum is very much a **working document**, not something to be kept on the top shelf. Its size, however, does make it difficult to transport so it is recommended that it is obtained in CD format and the parts needed most often can be printed off. Alternatively, divide the paper-based version into its different sections (one section per level) and incorporate the levels taught most often into a working file.

7

Building in sustainability

Good practice

Good teachers have always assessed and responded to their learners' needs. Procedures have, however, become more formalised as a result of government support for the sector through the *Skills for Life* strategy.

Good practice includes:

- initial and diagnostic assessment of learners;
- establishing and recording learners' goals;
- ongoing assessment which influences teaching and effective planning of learning;
- using information gained from assessment to draw up and review individual learning plans (ILPs);
- securing appropriate accreditation;
- ensuring progression;
- providing tutorial time and evaluating learning.

In order to meet the requirements of funders as well as Ofsted and the Adult Learning Inspectorate (ALI), tutors need to demonstrate that their teaching is effective and that learning is taking place. A key skill for tutors is to ensure that accurate records demonstrating progress and achievement are kept. ESOL learners are often highly mobile so it is important records are kept up to date, that systems are in place and everyone knows how to use them. This includes Level 2 and 3 staff with support roles. Records should be kept from the initial interview.

Promoting and defining achievement

Progress and achievement can be defined in many ways and should be interpreted more widely than qualifications. Adults also have other things they want to achieve in connection with their lives, which is why a holistic approach to planning is important when working with adult learners. Achievement needs to be defined by the learner and this may mean discussing what the learner wants to achieve, in their own language. It means recognising that ESOL learners have their own expectations and do not want to be continually identified as ESOL learners. Their goals may include wider social aims such as accessing services, developing an interest or joining a local group.

As a normal part of the teaching and tutoring teachers will consult with learners about topics that interest them and about their need to learn English. With absolute beginners, pictures can be used to help prompt the learners. As well as the linguistic aspects of negotiating this, there may be cultural differences that need to be taken account of. This procedure fulfils an important role by helping the learners to realise that, as adults, they are expected to have opinions abut what and how they learn. As adults they are also expected to take responsibility for making their learning successful. It may take time for some learners to understand this. Notions of learner empowerment may be new, especially if they appear to contradict expectations about classroom behaviour.

Effective assessment procedures should draw out learners' strengths as well as areas for development, including those in their first language. Achievable and realistic targets can then be set. Learners need to be challenged in order to demonstrate all the abilities they have. This means encouraging students to become active learners, both within and outside the classroom. It entails making use of all available resources that can be found in the environment around you: posters, leaflets, signs, letters, bills, menus, etc, and using contexts for learning which are relevant and meaningful to the lives of your learners. If you have access to computers, ICT skills can also be taught alongside the development of English language skills.

Initial assessment and placement of learners

When a learner arrives in a college or community centre, they will normally take part in an initial assessment. Many ESOL departments and schemes have devised their own initial assessment materials, which help to decide the best course or class for the learner. Using spoken English is usually a key part of initial assessment, generally as a discussion with learners about their learning. (See also ILPs).

Diagnostic assessment

After learners join a particular group or level, the tutor should work with learners to make a more in-depth assessment of their needs and abilities and agree targets for learning. This is called the diagnostic assessment.

Individual Learning Plans (ILPs)

This process enables the students to identify learning targets that are meaningful to them, and to subsequently review their progress with their tutor. In drawing up ILPs tutors need to consider both long- and medium-term aims and short-term targets. These are put together into an action plan that considers the skills, methods and the resources required. ILPs should be working documents, used as part of a process in which learners and tutors regularly review progress, record achievement and set new goals together. Parts of ILPs can be drawn up with whole groups of learners.

In some institutions, ILPs can become a contentious area for ESOL. This is because learners do not have the linguistic resources to negotiate the process. (Imagine devising an ILP for yourself in any language in which you are not very fluent.) Also, many ESOL learners do not come from cultures where the teacher seeks learners' views about their learning. At the earlier levels of ESOL, learners are usually prompted about their learning goals, although the content can be negotiated to accommodate particular interests. A problem too for ESOL tutors can be the size of classes, 15 or even up to 20 learners in a group are not uncommon.

Another issue around the use of Individual Learning Plans is when they are to be completed. Do they take up class time? Or should they be completed outside of regular class time?

The next stage after eliciting what the learners want to learn is to convert these broad aspirations into achievable targets, which both teacher and student can work towards.

The Lifeline on Embedded Literacy, Language and Numeracy Learning has a useful section on SMART targets. **SMART** = **S**pecific, **M**easurable, **A**chievable, **R**ealistic, **T**imebound

> **"I applaud ILPs in principle but it's very difficult in six hours a week to give a class (Entry 2) of 16 regular attenders sufficient time to discuss their goals individually with me. We do get some extra time for paper work and tutorials but it ends up with what we call 'gift time'. I have a regular weekly session where learners demonstrate to the whole class how they have achieved their learning goal for the week. It's small steps but I think it's working."**
> (Tutor)

ILPs help to track student progression, and the reviews require giving specific and detailed feedback to individual learners on their strengths and areas for further improvement. It can be very hard with some ESOL learners to make this process as meaningful as it is intended to be because of the barriers explained earlier.

It is possible to get achievement funding for targets achieved and recorded on learners' ILPs, as long as there is auditable proof (i.e. a written record of the process). Targets need to relate to the ESOL Core Curriculum. An ILP can demonstrate the individual's achievement in detail.

INSPIRATIONS

> Anh is from Vietnam and English pronunciation has always been difficult. On her ILP she identified her goal as reading a story book to her daughter. She brings in her book once a week and reads it to her group as evidence that she is achieving her goal. "It's proving very motivating," says her tutor.
> **(Community College tutor)**
>
> "In my Level 1 class I've got half the class writing their own SMART goals. They used to write things like, "I want to improve my writing and spelling." Now they are identifying little steps and I'm getting them to do things outside the classroom, like learning five new words a week. Diaries are less successful but I find spelling and word building tasks work well. Students will choose to write summaries of things seen on TV and that works well too."
> **(Community college tutor)**

There are debates around using ILPs on an individual basis with ESOL learners, and tutors should keep up to date with them.

Accreditation and qualifications for ESOL learners

This has been a rapidly changing area. The new ESOL accreditations have been mapped to the standards of the ESOL Curriculum. In addition, the Qualifications and Curriculum Authority (QCA) is working with the examining bodies to adapt the traditional accreditation for learners to the ESOL curriculum. It is important to match the learner to the qualification, rather than the reverse, especially as there are qualifications at all levels (from Pre-entry to Level 4) and for different skills.

The QCA requires examining boards to match their ESOL qualifications to the National Qualifications Framework (NQF). This means that tutors and learners can see how a particular qualification provides access to further qualifications and links with general and vocational qualifications.

Some exam boards assess learners through a portfolio of assignments and assessment is continuous. Other exam boards assess learners on their 'performance' in a nationally recognised test. Examining bodies are usually flexible and assessment can be held at a time and place convenient for the centre that is providing courses.

INSPIRATIONS

"We've put on a course called
Practical Crafts with OCN accreditation.
This year Floristry has taken off and we've got 8
students. It's an Entry unit and it matches really well to
the ESOL curriculum. The students love going on the visits
(so that brings in all the language for arranging travel too).
It's taught by a Malaysian tutor, with ESOL qualifications
who is also a florist. We were lucky to find someone
with both qualifications."
(Adult education ESOL manager)

For information on the new ESOL qualifications, which must be adopted from September 2004 see:

- http://www.dfes.gov.uk/readwriteplus/Learning
- http://www.qca.org.uk
- http://www.lifelonglearninguk.org

Progression

One of the best forms of evidence of student achievement is progression. Progression for ESOL learners takes many forms and apart from moving onto another ESOL course can include taking up other learning opportunities.

As ESOL qualifications are now achieved at levels which are part of the national qualifications framework (NQF), they should facilitate progression to other courses. This is particularly applicable to embedded courses where ESOL Entry 3 may form a pathway to either a preparatory subject linked course or to a Foundation level course with additional ESOL at Levels 1 and 2. Progression is now being much more widely defined than the next level of ESOL. However, level based ESOL courses are usually the backbone of an organisation's ESOL provision and many part-time learners are likely to experience progression to another ESOL class.

Mariam was born in Iran but she has lived over 10 years in the UK and could "get by" in most tasks that required English. She was motivated to enrol in an ESOL Literacy class at her local Adult Education Centre when she realised that her writing skills in English were worse than those of her seven year old son. Once she joined the class she progressed well and she realised that there were many other classes she could join at the Centre. By the end of the year she had completed the literacy class but then joined a hairdressing course and a "Prepare for Your Driving Test "class. This kind of progression is real achievement but ACL in the past has not always had robust systems for recording it.

There is a danger of adults being contained in courses that do not help them to progress into jobs that use the skills they have. ESOL learning should not be an end in itself.

As provision in a geographical area develops, closer working partnerships between different providers becomes essential if learners are to progress to different opportunities in line with goals they have identified for themselves. Managers of organisations need to put in place formal processes for facilitating co-operation between different providers to ensure learners have access to informed advice so that they can make choices. Ongoing advice and access to information, built into courses, is essential.

Consultation with learners and a sharp-eyed observation of changing life patterns are necessary on the part of ESOL managers so that progression may also involve responding to new needs.

With learners like Samina it is a lot easier to discuss their goals and give them the information to make informed choices for themselves than it is with learners whose English is very limited. Samina's story illustrates the importance of advice and guidance, of not seeing people solely in the role of ESOL learners and of understanding their aspirations.

INSPIRATIONS

> Samina is a refugee from Iraq who has a good level of English. She attended an Open Day at a university and asked about attending an intensive pre-sessional course so that she could enrol for a higher degree. When the course tutor asked her about her present studies she said she was attending an advanced ESOL course. She explained that her tutor there was encouraging her to enrol on an 'Introduction to Care' course which could lead to employment as a care assistant. The Higher Education course tutor asked if she wanted to become a care assistant. Samina said that was a hard decision to make because in Iraq she had been a university professor and she really wanted to use her specialist knowledge here and retrain in her subject.

Tutorials

The function of tutorials needs to be very clear: that they are to support the learners' learning, not her/his personal needs. New arrivals in the UK may have many pressing needs and ESOL teachers can argue that, until the learners' basic needs are met how can they tackle the demanding task of learning another language? However, the ESOL teacher is not there to sort out personal problems such as the learners' housing benefit but to give the student the knowledge and the communication skills to sort it out for him or her self. Part of the ESOL tutor's role is to know when and how to refer learners to appropriate sources of support.

Regular tutorials reveal a lot of learners' real motivations for learning and help teachers to encourage learners not just to 'get by' but to 'get on'.

Evaluating courses

Most adult education schemes carry out regular paper-based consultations with their learners asking them to evaluate their class and the service as a whole. For Entry 1 and 2 ESOL learners this process may have little meaning. ESOL teachers need to include the language of review and evaluation in their classroom teaching. Some tutors use a process of evaluating learning which starts by providing lots of support and gradually encourages more and more independence. For example, at Entry 3, a learning journal (or similar) can be completed initially as a group composition but eventually as an independent activity. This approach is known as 'scaffolding'.

In the Medway Adult and Community Learning Service, an Education Adviser asks all ESOL enquirers about their goals and identifies with them the steps needed to gain, for example, their driving licence or become a nurse. Individuals are referred on to other provision (such as the local FE college, or specialist services) where appropriate. Few adult education services appear to offer such a service.

INSPIRATIONS

The service received funding from NIACE to run more community based provision. Five former learners from that project are now preparing to be Learning Support Assistants in local schools. The ESOL tutor is in a support role and joins the learners in the class but isn't involved in teaching them herself. In the afternoon she runs a group tutorial with them and helps them to prepare evidence for their portfolios. One has already got a job (in February) for September and local schools are reportedly very keen to employ them.

"These are women who were in a class at the local Gurdwara a year ago and had never walked into an ESOL class. Without the project we wouldn't have reached them and look where they are going now. Once they get the chance some students learn very fast." (ESOL Curriculum leader, Medway Adult and Community Learning Service)

Keeping records

In order to meet the requirements of funders and inspection, records should be kept which track learners' progress through their learning programme(s).

Here are some suggestions of what to record:

- Learners' achievement on entry (screening forms and/or initial assessment results);
- Results of diagnostic assessment activities;
- Progress and achievement against short-term targets and long-term goals as set out in the ILP. This should include self-report and can relate also to activities outside of the formal programme of study;
- Progression onto non-ESOL courses, learners doing other things (getting a job).

Ideally, records should also be kept of activities relating to staff development; resources, materials and equipment purchased and used; and any time spent on additional, unpaid activities with learners.

INSPIRATIONS

The Entry 1 class in this East Midlands town is taught by a young man with an EFL background. His students range in age from 18–58; they include two young men from Columbia with a background in trade Union activism, an older women from Argentina who is an Evangelical Christian, a young mother from Saudi Arabia who attends class in full burqa with only her eyes showing, a Spanish chef , a young Indian bride whose father-in-law is prominent in the management of the local Hindu temple, and a young worker from Hong Kong with significant pronunciation problems.

Predictable barriers of age, gender, religion, culture and language are overcome in the emergence of a learning group. They are a cohesive group. They move around working with different people. Where there is a language in common they use it to help with the English but they explain to their colleagues what they are saying. During the course of the lesson everyone tries out their English. This does not happen by accident. If someone runs out of words during a roleplay other students will prompt them. If someone is absent, another student will volunteer to contact them to find out what is wrong. When the tutor shows some of the classes' written work on the overhead projector, the students compete to find the mistakes but when individual students made speeches for their English Speaking Board examination the others in the audience were able to express their appreciation. They greet each other in the way in use in their respective countries. (Observer)

Many people who want to learn English want to learn it fast – in order to get that desperately needed job or to progress to a college course in September. What about intensive one-week courses? Or courses on Sundays because it's the only day some learners are not working? Some organisations have been running such courses for years but in others a new ESOL manager may find real resistance to change from ESOL tutors as well as managers.

(Consultant and trainer)

As learners perceive they are being helped to succeed at things they want to do, they become more prepared to reveal other goals. Organisations who have taken seriously the notion that ESOL is about encouraging learners to communicate what they want, have found that motivation and commitment to learning also increased.

> When many of the male ESOL learners in Blackburn Adult Education College worked double day shifts in textile mills, ESOL classes were arranged on a double shift pattern as well so that learners came one week in the morning and one week in the afternoon.

Flexibility and imagination in the management of provision are likely to maximize students' learning. Above all, it is necessary to look for ways of recognising achievement all of the time.

INSPIRATIONS

Case Study – progression in a rural area (North Yorkshire)

It is important to remember what learners are in ESOL classes for. When North Yorkshire Community Education wanted to investigate the learning needs of black and ethnic minority adults living in Ryedale 15 of the 25 adults contacted came through links with ESOL learning. But the success of the project was measured in far wider terms than language attainment.

"Support was provided for one of the participants who did not feel confident enough and lacked access to training and job opportunities. She had a Thai background and previous experience as a hairdresser. Contacts were facilitated through the local network and she has been able to gain employment as a hairdresser, learn English, meet people and has become part of the community."

"An Eastern European woman who was unemployed, has improved her English, obtained a job and passed the driving theory test."

8 ESOL and social inclusion

ESOL learners with learning difficulties and disabilities

A key theme of the *Skills for Life* strategy is ensuring inclusion for all learners. There is now an ESOL version of the Access for All guidance in draft and materials are being piloted in selected projects. The final guidance document should be available after July 2005.

Dyslexia

How to deal with dyslexia requires specialist training. For more advice search the Internet for organisations with expertise and experience of appropriate learning approaches for ESOL learners who may be dyslexic. Also www.dyslexic.com for advice and information on resources.

See the Bibliography section for *Dyslexia and the Bilingual Learner*, published by (L)LLU (London) Language and Literacy Unit.

Accreditation for learners with learning difficulties and disabilities

NOCN's (National Open College Network) policy on special assessment arrangements is helpful and describes special arrangements that can be made for Open College Networks (OCN) learners. Contact your local OCN if you want to know more about the NOCN Qualification Guide for ESOL. NOCN qualification number: FK2LOQ002).

The DfES Contextualised *Skills for Life Guide for Adult and Community Learning* Resources Section gives details of some useful DfES publications.

Bilingual adults who want to learn to read and write

A small but significant number of bilingual adults with fluent oral skills are in ESOL programmes because an adult literacy manager may say they can't place them in a literacy group. While the ESOL tutor usually finds a way of responding to them and the learner is usually initially happy, their needs are probably not best met. This is particularly so if they see themselves as having more in common with people who don't have a problem with using spoken English in their daily lives. We do not know how many such learners there are and unless an organisation develops a strategy, like having a language policy, such learners will continue to fall between two parallel forms of provision. Under the *Skills for Life* strategy, literacy volunteers and tutors need to know how to support learners who may be fluent in spoken English but through no fault of their own, have never become literate in any language. Volunteers also need to understand the range and variety of spoken English and how this may affect how speakers of non-standard English are perceived.

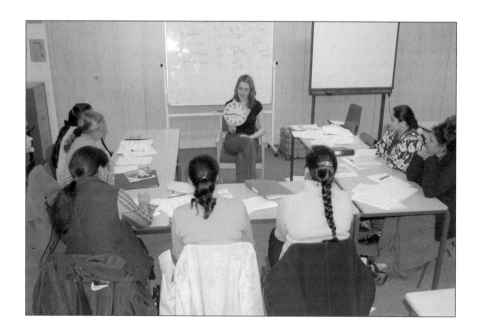

9 Partnerships and collaboration

All successful ESOL providers work within networks which may include education providers; statutory and voluntary organisations; cultural and religious groups; higher education institutions; local and national professional networks; and arts and the media. It is probably one of the aspects of ESOL work that makes involvement challenging and fun. However, for the newcomer to the field there are ways of learning from others and discovering where particular strengths and interests are without having to learn everything through experience.

The DfES support pack *Working with Refugees and Asylum Seekers* (2003) is full of invaluable advice about how to do things and has an excellent section, with a proforma, on developing local networks. This is a good starting point for anyone new to the field and also has useful reminders and current information for experienced staff .

Sue Harris, Head of ESOL at Adult Education College Bexley, regularly monitors her local target group. "My latest research [2004] shows a significant increase in the proportion of European ESOL Learners. The influx of refugees from the Balkans and Eastern Europe contributed to this, together with the growing number of EU/EEA migrant workers. Monitoring changes over time in the student body helps identify gaps in provision and informs future planning. For example, we found that there were more learners who were working so we opened more evening classes. We have a large number of Chinese restaurants in the area and their staff have very limited time off, restricted to Mondays. We have now set up a Monday morning English workshop for Chinese restaurant staff so that they have a convenient opportunity to learn relevant language skill: not just general everyday communication but also topics that will help in their work. An awareness of your area's demographic profile, the local labour market and skills shortages and maintaining a network of local contacts help bids for funding projects with ethnic minority and refugee groups."

The other NIACE Lifelines, particularly those on community education, give useful insights into developing work outside formal learning organisations. *Community Education and Neighbourhood Renewal*, (Thompson, 2002) and *Working with Asian Heritage Communities* (McNulty, 2003) are particularly relevant.

Working within the organisation

Working within an organisation information flows up as well as down and all ESOL staff can contribute ideas and contacts for local networking that lead to new courses and other provision being developed. It's important to attend training events and meetings in order to feel part of the organisation. Tutors should be entitled to be paid to attend such events and most organisations do offer to meet at least part of the cost.

Working with each other and peer review are becoming important as a way of encouraging practitioners to think more deeply about what they do.

"We need to improve the quality of teaching and learning in the classroom and, as tutors ourselves, to use the Common Inspection Framework and work with each other; in peer observations for example, to review and improve the quality of teaching practice." (Tutor)

Working outside your organisation

It is very useful to research local minority ethnic populations, their scale and type of need.

The following are examples of the kind of links ESOL managers develop. These networks can come together to develop local initiatives, run conferences together and contribute to training events. They are also a good way of finding out whether there are emerging needs for new courses. They can be useful for identifying progression routes for learners into training for work and college courses.

Local links:

- Statutory agencies: education, especially schools and colleges; health; housing; DHSS; youth and community services; libraries.
- Voluntary organisations: Race Equality Councils (RECs); community groups; cultural and religious centres; groups for pre-school children and for older people; clubs and societies.
- Business and industry: training organisations; work-based learning; union representatives.

10 Check it out

- ESOL learners bring with them a range of experiences of life as well as education. Use this richness and diversity to plan meaningful and interesting learning activities.
- Remember that the student usually has to negotiate their learning in English rather than in their first language. Frontline or reception staff can gain a Level 2 qualification to help them support and respond sensitively to ESOL learners.
- Follow the ESOL Curriculum and *Skills for Life* guidelines on initially assessing and reviewing and placing learners on a course. Work with learners to make the process of assessment and review of targets as meaningful as possible.
- Use the ESOL curriculum as a framework to structure learning and use it creatively so that learners' real needs are responded to.
- Use (and develop) qualified staff who can give advice and know where to refer people to.
- Provide courses with clear objectives. Agree topics and themes with learners (at all levels and types of provision).
- Progression should be supported within and between different forms of provision within local communities, ESOL and beyond to vocational and professional opportunities, further and higher education, etc.
- Access staff training and development to meet new challenges and overcome gaps in existing staffing.
- Keeping records may seem like an additional burden but they are essential evidence that public money is being spent appropriately and can help support an organisation's case for further development. Use the DfES Contextualised Guides (See Bibliography).
- Make maximum use of help from other colleagues and services and do not ever believe it is possible to work entirely alone.

11 Issues and challenges

1) Migration, citizenship and language may be hugely challenging areas for governments, society and education, but see them as positive challenges!

2) The history of ESOL learning shows that we are in a period of unprecedented expansion and growth for ESOL (alongside teachers of literacy and numeracy). We need to face these challenges and use the opportunities of change to ensure that learners have every chance to fulfil their potential.

3) There are additional costs for staffing and staff development which need to be met:
   - paid time for tutorials;
   - allocated meeting time for CPD, development work and designing new courses;
   - the demands of additional paperwork especially for hourly paid tutors in adult and community education.

4) Some tutors have low expectations of ESOL learners and some managers have low expectations of tutors. We shouldn't assume that 'Entry level' English means low-level skills in language, literacy or general education in learners.

5) Discrete ESOL courses may not be appropriate for all learners. While the expansion of specialist ESOL courses is necessary, it is also important to find new ways of supporting ESOL learners on other courses. Vocational tutors need support and appropriate professional development/training to enable them to support ESOL learners effectively on mainstream courses.

6) The pressures on ESOL tutors have always been considerable. There is also a long-standing tension between teaching with a focus on English grammar and understanding what learners want and need to learn in order to get on with their lives. The Curriculum standards for ESOL relieve some of these pressures, although they also demand greater accountability over what is taught. Managers should ensure that tutors have continuing opportunities for professional development so that they can keep up to date with policy and good practice.

7) ESOL is an extraordinarily varied and continuously changing field to work in and this makes it simultaneously both challenging and satisfying. There are always new ideas to be understood and absorbed. Finding opportunities to work with others is one of the best ways of continuing to improve our practice.

"I feel I am very much part of the learning process, I am a learner too and I don't say that in a rhetorical way at all... I aspire to be an intelligent professional. To me a model of an intelligent professional is one that is always learning. And I try to fit in with that idea. I learn from every instance of my teaching; I learn from the errors, from the successes... I learn from the students and I'm not trying to pretend I'm being humble because I'm not." (Tutor and course co-ordinator)

The opportunity that faces ESOL practitioners now is to break down the barriers that have contained both themselves and ESOL learners. Our task is to help learners achieve the necessary command of English that will encourage them to succeed at a level that matches their history and expectations both within and more importantly, outside the ESOL classroom.

Bibliography and resources

Barton, D. and Pitt, K. (2003), *Research Review: Adult ESOL pedagogy: a review of research, an annotated bibliography and recommendations for future research.* London, NRDC (Can be downloaded as a PDF document)

BSA and ACLF, (2003), *Basic Skills and Refugees* (produced with the Refugee Council.) London. A free booklet that has straightforward information and an extremely useful list of organisations, with full details of how to contact them and an explanation of what they do. It can be used by people who want the information for themselves and also as a source of reference by advice workers.

BSA and NRDC, (2003), *Using laptop computers to develop basic skills: a handbook for practitioners.* BSA/NRDC (Can be downloaded from NRDC site)

Department for Education and Skills (2003), *Working with Refugees and Asylum Seekers: support material for ESOL practitioners.* Available from DfES publications, Prolog. Tel: 0845 6022260. Produced for ESOL providers as a file of support materials. It gives advice on setting up and delivering ESOL provision, training materials and has a wealth of case studies to explain and illustrate the main points. It has advice on resources, websites and sources for up-to-date statistics.

Department for Education and Skills (2002), *Access for All: guidance on making the adult literacy and numeracy core curricula accesssible.* LSDA/DfES

Department for Education and Employment (2000), *Breaking the Language Barriers: report of the working group on English for Speakers of Other Languages (ESOL).* DfEE Ref: Contact email: dfes@prolog.uk.com

Dubin, F. and Olshtain, E. (1992), *Course Design, Developing Programs and Materials for Language Learning.* Cambridge, CUP

Frow, M. (1996) *Roots of the Future.* London, Commission for Racial Equality

Jordan, J. (third edition,1998), *An Introduction to teaching English as an Additional Language for Adults*. London, BSA. (Out of print but very useful for inexperienced tutors)

Kambouri, M., Toutounji, I and Francis, H, (1995), *Drop out and Progression from ESOL Provision*. London, BSA

McNulty, D. (2003), *Working with Asian heritage communities*. NIACE, Leicester.

Molteno, M. (1987), *A Language in Common*. London, The Women's Press

Nicholls, S. and Hoadley-Maidment, E. eds.(1991), *Current Issues in Teaching English as a Second Language to Adults*. Nelson

Robson, M., (1987), *Language, Learning and Race*. Further Education Unit/ Longman (Out of print)

Schellekens, P. (2001), *English as a Barrier to Employment, Education and Training*. DfES research doc. 4RP/21098

Sunderland, H., Klein, C., Savinson, R., and Partridge, T., (1997), *Dyslexia and the Bilingual Learner: assessing and teaching adults and young people who speak English as an additional language*. London, London Language and Literacy Unit at South Bank University.

Thompson, J. (2002), C*ommunity Education and Neighbourhood Renewal*. NIACE, Leicester

Ufi (University for Industry) (2002). *Using ICT to Develop Literacy and Numeracy: a guide for learning centres working with adult learners*. Report available from Ufi research team: www.learndirect.co.uk

ESOL within the *Skills for Life* initiative

Department for Education and Skills (2001). *Adult ESOL Core Curriculum CD ROM + Access for All (CDALCC)*. Contact Basic Skills Agency: 0870 600 2400

Department for Education and Employment/FENTO (2002), *Subject Specifications for teachers of Adult Literacy and Numeracy* Ref: DfES/SSO1/2002. Contact email: dfes@prolog.uk.com

Department for Education and Skills (2003), *The Skills for Life Teaching Qualifications Framework: a users guide*. DfES, London

Department for Education and Skills, *Inspection Guides* – Five publications giving guidance on the inspection of literacy, numeracy and ESOL Provision (SFL IG)

Department for Education and Skills (2002), *Success in Adult Literacy, Numeracy and ESOL Provision: a guide to support the Common Inspection framework*. (DfES/GCIF 02/2002)

Department for Education and Skills (2004), *Raising Standards – Adult and Community Learning: a guide to help providers achieve excellence for learners in Adult and Community Learning (SFLACL)*. DfES Publications. There are nine contextualised guides in this very useful series.

Department for Education and Skills (2004), *Planning Learning and Recording Progress and Achievement: a guide for practitioners*. DfES, Nottingham

Department for Education and Skills (2003), *Removing the Barriers* (Ref. 0001/2002, DfES publications: dfes@prolog.uk.com

Learning Materials Teacher Pack for ESOL (SfL TPLM/E)

Diagnostic Assessment Pack for ESOL (DAM3) + CD-ROM (DAM6)

FENTO (2003), *Guidance on using the Subject Specifications for teachers of English for Speakers of Other Languages (ESOL) at Level 4 in conjunction with the Standards for teaching and supporting learning*. FENTO Ref:DfES/SPESOL/2003

Articles

Schellekens, P. 'Individual Learning Plans: fit for purpose' in *Reflect*, the magazine of the NRDC, Oct 2004. (*Reflect* is a free magazine for LLN practitioners, phone 020 7612 6476 or e-mail info@nrdc.org.uk)

Sunderland, H. and Wilkins, M. 'ILPs in ESOL; theory, research and practice' in *Reflect*, Oct 2004.

Frank, F. 'Backwards to the Future' in *Basic Skills Bulletin*, November 2003

Sickling, T. 'Action for Inclusion' in *Basic Skills Bulletin*, March 2003 issue 11
The Basic Skills Bulletin basicskills@circa-uk.demon.co.uk, Phone: 01223 564334

Burdon, S. and Guneri, G. 'Moving from TEFL to TESOL' iatefl (International Association of Teachers of English as a Foreign Language), p. 2 in *IATEFL Special Interest Group newsletter*, Issue 1, Autumn 2003.

ESOL reference books

Collins Cobuild English Dictionary (1995), (University of Birmingham with Collins Cobuild), Glasgow, Harper Collins

Crystal, D., (1998) *Rediscover Grammar*, Harlow, Longman

Department for Education and Skills (2003), *Working with Refugees and Asylum Seekers*. Section 4 provides guidance on developing a programme for refugees

Harmer, J. (1998), *How to Teach English*. Longman

Harmer, J. (April 2004), *How to teach Writing*. Longman

Swan, M. and Smith, B. (2001) *Learner English*. Cambridge, CUP (Analyses learners' languages in relation to English)

Swan, M. (1995), *Practical English Usage*. Oxford, OUP

Back numbers of *Language Issues* available from NATECLA National Centre. The most accessible way of keeping up to date with current theories about ESOL and often have information about other languages not covered in 'Learner English'.

Miscellaneous

DfES (2003)*Working Together: Connexions supporting young asylum seekers and refugees* (Ref CXDIFFREF). Available from: dfes@prolog.uk.com

ALI /Ofsted Inspection reports
Readers who are interested in how good practice is being defined in ESOL should keep up to date with the latest inspection Reports on Colleges, ACLs and Training Providers. Read the ones where ESOL has been awarded a Grade 1 or 2.

ESOL materials

Worksheets for Beginners – ESOL Literacy and Listening for Beginners, both published by Cardiff County Council

Listening for Beginners by Helen Adams

Friends, Families and Folktales, Language and Literacy Unit, South Bank University

The ESOL Literacy Pack, Lisa Karlsen. Oxford Basics series, OUP

Writing Works, An LLU+ publication, available from Avanti Books (www.avantibooks.com)

Visual, oral, aural and written resources

Films, songs, novels, expressive and visual art forms provide insights into cultures and experiences that ESOL tutors will find interesting and relevant. The potential list is huge and the opportunities for discovery and enjoyment are well worth seeking out.

The Museum of Immigration and Diversity
19 Princelet Street, London
Tel: 020 7247 5352
Website: www.19.princelet street.org.uk

www.movinghere a website on the history of four well established settler groups: Jewish, Irish, Afro-Caribbean, South Asian, built up from oral history archives across the country

Visram R. (1986), *Ayahs, Lascars and Princes, The Story of Indians in Britain 1700-1947*, Pluto Press

Marantos, C. and Rickard, R. (1990), *The Pashtuns of Aylesbury: a brief study of a Pakistani community* (written in collaboration with the Pashtun community). Buckinghamshire County Council

Readers may be able to find sources for the migration history of other groups who have been significant in their own areas e.g. Yemenis in Sheffield, Chinese in Liverpool, Punjabi Sikhs in Gravesend. Local museums are often a good place to start.

Useful websites, organisations and contacts

The Home Office
http://www.ind.homeoffice.gov.uk/

Department for Education and Skills publications
dfes@prolog.uk.com

Department for Education and Skills ReadWritePlus website
www.dfes.gov.uk/readwriteplus

National Research and Development Centre for adult literacy and numeracy
http://www.nrdc.org.uk

Basic Skills Agency Resource Centre
http://www.ioe.ac.uk/library/bsa

The Basic Skills Agency
http://www.basic-skills.co.uk

The Refugee Council
www.refugeecouncil.org.uk

The National Association for Teaching English and Other Community Languages to Adults
www.natecla.org.uk

Eflweb
www.eflweb.com

Organisations

National Association for the Teaching of English and other Community Languages to Adults (NATECLA) www.natecla.org.uk

International Association for the Teaching of English as a Foreign Language (IATEFL) generalenquiries@iatefl.org or 01227 824430

Useful contacts

The National Research and Development Centre (for Literacy, Numeracy and Language), Institute of Education, University of London, 20 Bedford Way, London, WC1H 0AL
Tel. 020 7612 6476, email: info@nrdc.org.uk Web: www.nrdc.org.uk

The Basic Skills Agency Resource Centre, Institute of Education Library, 20 Bedford Way, London, WC1 0AL
Tel. 020 7612 6069 (see Basic Skills, summer 2003 for Barbara Sakyra's article) b.sakyra@ioe.co.uk www.ioe.ac.uk/library/bsa

The Refugee Council: 020 7737 1155. Advice line: 020 736 6777

Talent, the online community for everyone involved in adult literacy, ESOL and numeracy: talent.ac.uk

Glossary

Differentiation: treating learners according to their individual learning needs

Gurdwara: a Sikh temple

Holistic: seeing learners as 'whole people' rather than as students of a subject

Inclusion: Policies to ensure people are included rather than left out or treated differently

Learndirect: a government initiative to promote on-line learning. www.learndirect.co.uk

Literacies: recognising that literacy takes many forms including visual communication, ICT and in languages apart from English. Also within English literacy there are different forms which are dependent on social contexts

Received pronunciation or Standard English: the regional British accent traditionally associated with educated speech (also known as BBC English)

Spiky profile: a common feature of ESOL learners where attainment in certain language skills may be considerably higher than attainment in others. E.g. one student may speak fluent colloquial English but be unable to write a single sentence, another may be able to read the text book but not participate in informal conversation.

Words about education and its institutions

ACL	Adult and Community Learning
ALI	Adult Learning Inspectorate
BSA	Basic Skills Agency
CRE	Commission for Racial Equality
DfES	Department for Education and Skills

EAL	(English as an additional language) This term is used in schools provision
FE	Further Education
FENTO	Further Education National Training Organisation
ILEA	Inner London Education Authority
LLLU	London Language and Literacy Unit (South Bank University)
LSA	Learning Skills Agency
LSDA	Learning Skills Development Agency
NATECLA	National Association for Teachers of English and other Community Languages to Adults
NIACE	National Institute for Adult and Community Education
NRDC	National Research and Development Centre
Ofsted	A branch of this inspectorate is responsible for all 16-19 education
Section 11	LEAs had to apply for funding by making their case and undertaking to meet 25% of the teacher's salary
Skills for Life	the national strategy for improving adult literacy and numeracy skills